drug facts
ECSTASY

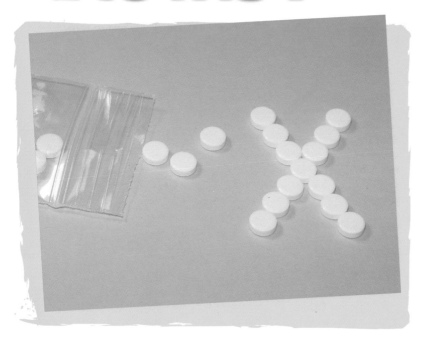

SUZANNE LEVERT with Jeff Hendricks

Marshall Cavendish
Benchmark
New York

Marshall Cavendish Benchmark
99 White Plains Road
Tarrytown, NY 10591
www.marshallcavendish.us

All websites were available and accurate when this book was sent to press.

Library of Congress Cataloging-in-Publication Data

LeVert, Suzanne.
  Ecstasy / by Suzanne LeVert with Jeff Hendricks.
    p. cm. — (Benchmark rockets : drug facts)
  Includes index.
  Summary: "Discusses the history, effects, and dangers of Ecstasy as well as addiction treatment options"—Provided by publisher.
    ISBN 978-0-7614-4349-0
1. Ecstasy (Drug)—Juvenile literature. 2. Designer drugs—Juvenile literature. 3. Drug abuse—Juvenile literature. I. Hendricks, Jeff. II. Title.

HV5822.M38L48 2010
613.8'3—dc22
2008052753

Publisher: Michelle Bisson
Editorial Development and Book Design: Trillium Publishing, Inc.

Photo research by Trillium Publishing, Inc.

Cover photo: Drug Enforcement Administration

The photographs and illustrations in this book are used by permission and through the courtesy of: iStockphoto.com: sx70, 1; Stockphoto4u, 12; Aldo Murillo, 27. Shutterstock.com: Dario Diament, 4; Sebastian Kaulitzki, 13, 14; Tracy Whiteside, 16; Jack Dagley Photography, 22; Rui Vale de Sousa, 23; Yuri Arcurs, 26. Drug Enforcement Administration: 10, 17. Corbis: Tom Stewart, 24.

Printed in Malaysia
1 3 5 6 4 2

CONTENTS

1 Club Drugs: The X Factor

IF YOU HAVE BEEN TO A DANCE CLUB OR A **RAVE**, you have probably heard about Ecstasy. Or maybe you heard about a drug called *E, Love, X, Adam*, or *Eve*. These are some nicknames for Ecstasy. Its scientific name is *methylenedioxymethamphetamine*, or *MDMA* for short. But people commonly call this drug *Ecstasy*, due to the feelings of **ecstasy** it can create.

Ecstasy has been popular among teenagers since it was introduced into American culture in the 1990s. Nearly 9 percent of high school students have tried Ecstasy. The percentage of college students is even higher. But what is this drug, and why is it so popular?

Ecstasy is know as a "club drug" due to its popularity at dance clubs and raves.

What Is Ecstasy?

Many illegal drugs come from nature. For example, cocaine comes from the coca leaf. Marijuana is grown from hemp plants. Heroin is made from the poppy flower. But Ecstasy is different. Ecstasy is a **designer drug**. This means it's made in labs and designed for certain results. Ecstasy is a combination of drugs that act like **stimulants** and drugs that act like **hallucinogens**. The result is a high with two sides.

Because Ecstasy is part stimulant, someone who takes it is likely to feel a rise in blood pressure, heart rate, and energy level. At the same time, the hallucinogen-like qualities of the drug make users feel as if all of their senses are clearer and stronger than usual. Sensations may seem more intense. The drug creates a sense of well-being. Users often describe feeling relaxed and confident. They may feel more open, compassionate, and **empathetic**.

But Ecstasy has another side. The high that draws people to the drug can also lead to dangers, such as unsafe rises in body temperature and heart rate. Thousands of people are sent to the emergency room each year as a result of using this drug. Using Ecstasy can also lead to risky behaviors. The feelings of openness and compassion that the drug creates can confuse a user's sense of right and wrong. This has led many users to engage in risky sexual behaviors.

After people come down from their high, they often feel sick and tired. Many feel guilt and regret. Long-term use can cause memory loss, **depression**, and other medical problems. And even casual use can cause death.

Uses and Popularity

Ecstasy was invented by a German drug company in 1914. Research was done on the drug in the 1970s, when it was given to patients in therapy. The patients who took Ecstasy were able to be more open about their feelings. This made their therapy sessions more useful. Used in this way, the drug was helpful.

Today, researchers are looking again at using Ecstasy in therapy. They want to see if Ecstasy can help people who have been through major **traumas**. Many times, people suffer greatly after a trauma. They have flashbacks, nightmares, depression, **anxiety**, and guilt. Researchers give trauma patients Ecstasy in its purest form. The patients take Ecstasy while with a doctor or therapist. Current research suggests that Ecstasy is very helpful when used this way. Not everyone supports these tests, however. This is due to the fact that Ecstasy is an illegal drug in the United States.

Teenagers may feel this drug is helpful to them, too, in that it provides a break from things that are difficult for them. For example, Ecstasy can make people feel self-confident. This feeling may be appealing to teens, who often struggle with issues of self-esteem.

The price of Ecstasy is another reason it is popular with young people. Ecstasy is sold in tablets. One tablet of Ecstasy costs about $20. So, for the price of pizza and a movie, people can buy a high that lasts from two to five hours.

So how did this old drug gain new popularity? It happened soon after it came to American dance clubs in the 1990s. Right away, people liked the way Ecstasy made the loud music and flashing lights more intense. As the rave culture spread across the United States, the popularity of Ecstasy grew.

Today, ravers are not the only people who take Ecstasy. Ecstasy use has spread from dance parties to college campuses and into high schools and even middle schools.

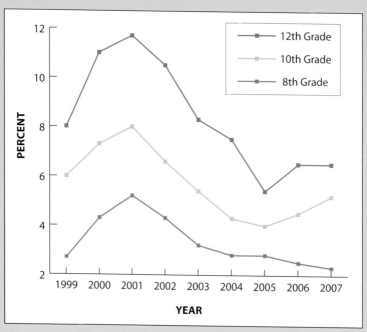

Percentage of U.S. Students Who Report Having Used Ecstasy at Least Once

Source: The Monitoring the Future Study, 2008

Ecstasy and Other Drugs

A tablet of Ecstasy is hardly ever pure. Most Ecstasy tablets contain other drugs, including some that are even more dangerous than Ecstasy.

In a research study published in 2000, scientists examined over one hundred tablets of Ecstasy. An organization called DanceSafe had secretly provided these tablets to the scientists. The lab results showed that nearly one-third of the tablets were not even Ecstasy. They were other drugs. And more than half of the tablets contained a mixture of Ecstasy and other drugs.

The other drug that they most often found was something commonly used in over-the-counter cough syrups. However, in the Ecstasy tablets, this drug was used in much larger amounts than are ever used in cough syrup. Such large amounts of an otherwise helpful drug can have serious, negative side effects, including mood swings, irregular heartbeat, and anxiety.

The problem of impure Ecstasy is made worse due to the fact that young people often use Ecstasy with other illegal drugs on purpose. It is fairly common to take Ecstasy with alcohol, marijuana, or other **club drugs**. These combinations can increase the negative effects of Ecstasy.

Other Club Drugs

Official Name	Nickname	Some Side Effects
Fentanyl	Dance fever, jackpot	Breathing slows down or stops
GHB (Gamma-hydroxybutyrate)	G, liquid Ecstasy	Headaches, passing out, uncontrollable shaking (seizures), coma, death
Ketamine	Special K	Increased heart rate, memory loss, seizures, risk of heart attack
LSD	Acid, L, Lucy in the Sky with Diamonds	Anxiety, nausea, believing in things that are not true, seeing things that are not there
Rohypnol	Roofie, roche	Light-headedness, drowsiness, lack of muscle control

2 Your Body and Brain on Ecstasy

YOUR BODY KNOWS WHEN ECSTASY IS IN YOUR SYSTEM. Ecstasy will make your heart beat faster and your blood pressure rise. This leads to some of the more uncomfortable side effects of this drug, such as a rapid heartbeat, breathlessness, and tiredness. It can also lead to permanent damage and heart attacks in people with heart problems.

Ecstasy causes additional changes in the body. One common side effect is the uncontrollable clenching of the teeth. This is why Ecstasy users suck on pacifiers or lollipops. Ecstasy also raises a person's body temperature, causing sweating and thirst. This is why most Ecstasy users will drink a lot of water. This is also why, at some dance parties, there may be a separate room that is cooler than the main party room.

Tablets of Ecstasy come in different shapes and colors and with different stamps. All tablets of Ecstasy affect brain chemistry.

Ecstasy affects the mind and emotions of users, too. Researchers have found that heavy users display a wide range of serious emotional problems, such as unreasonable and uncontrollable worry, anger, and fear. Using Ecstasy often leads to problems with sleep and short-term and long-term memory problems. Ecstasy users become more likely to act without thinking, too. And immediate illness, permanent brain damage, and even death can result from just one large **dose** of Ecstasy.

Doses and Overdoses

Research makes it clear that the more Ecstasy a person takes, the greater the danger is to his or her body and mind. One thing that makes this particularly worrisome is that it is easy for a person to take more Ecstasy than he or she planned to. This is because the strength of a single dose of Ecstasy can vary greatly. Tablets that look the same can have anywhere from 50 to 300 milligrams of Ecstasy in them.

A dose of about 100 milligrams lasts from three to six hours. A dose of 300 milligrams might last three times that long.

Getting more than you bargained for becomes even more likely when taking multiple tablets of Ecstasy at one time or over a period of time. This happens when users experiment with "stacking," or taking three or more tablets at once. Another risky thing people have tried is "piggybacking," or taking a series of tablets over a period of time. When people experiment like this, or anytime people use Ecstasy, they run the risk of **overdose**.

Symptoms of an Ecstasy overdose include the following:

- Nausea
- Difficulty talking
- Vomiting
- Inability to sweat
- Racing heartbeat, even while at rest
- Fainting
- Uncontrollable shaking or twitching
- Loss of muscle control
- Problems urinating
- High blood pressure
- Muscle cramping
- High body temperature
- Kidney failure

Anyone can suffer an Ecstasy overdose.

It Begins in the Brain

The results of Ecstasy are clear. But how does Ecstasy create these results? Ecstasy acts on the brain to change the chemistry in it.

Your brain is responsible for controlling all of the functions of your body. It controls basic tasks, such as your heart rate and breathing. The brain also controls more complex tasks, such as thought, memory, and speech. Every emotion you feel and every action you take begins in the brain. Messages are communicated from the brain to the body through **nerve fibers**. These fibers travel down your spine and throughout your body.

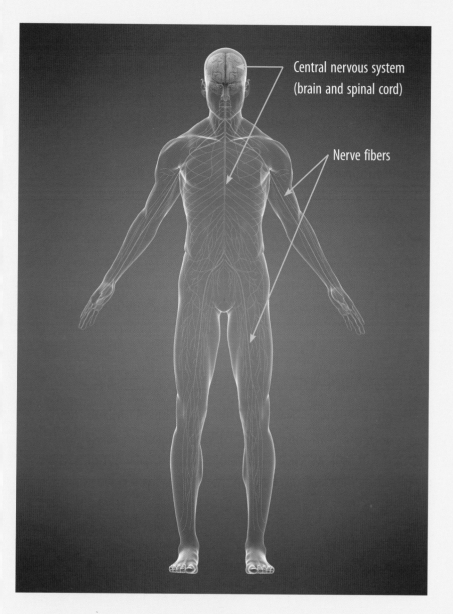

Central nervous system
(brain and spinal cord)

Nerve fibers

There are 31 pairs of nerve fibers that carry messages from the brain to the skin, muscles, organs, and glands and then back. They work with the central nervous system—the brain and the spinal cord—to control tasks such as thinking, remembering, feeling, and moving.

Getting the Message Across

The messages from your brain travel from one nerve cell to another at fantastic speeds. But between each nerve cell is a tiny gap. To get across this gap, a message needs help. It gets this help from natural body chemicals called **neurotransmitters**. Neurotransmitters act like tiny river rafts, carrying messages from one nerve cell to the nerve cell on the other side of the gap.

Different neurotransmitters carry different types of messages, and the messages affect different actions and feelings. For example, one neurotransmitter helps control appetite and heart rate. Another controls moods. A different one helps during times of stress. Neurotransmitters must be present in the right amounts and in the right balance for the human brain to work properly. Using Ecstasy messes up the balance of these chemicals.

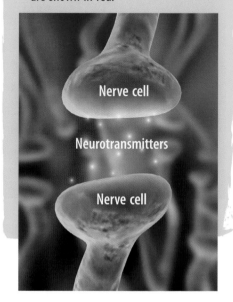

Messages from and to the brain pass across the gap between two nerve cells. The neurotransmitters are shown in red.

Nerve cell

Neurotransmitters

Nerve cell

Will the Body or Mind *Need* Ecstasy?

Some drugs, such as heroin or cocaine, lead quickly to **addictions**. An addiction can be defined as when someone does at least three of the following things for one year or longer:

• Takes more of a drug than they meant to take

• Takes the drug for a longer period of time than they meant to

• Has tried to use less of the drug and failed

• Spends a lot of time getting the drug, using the drug, or recovering from the effects of the drug

• Misses out on important events because of drug use

• Keeps using a drug that causes problems in the body or mind

• Keeps using a drug that makes problems in the body or mind worse

Ecstasy does not seem to create addictions as easily as drugs like heroin and cocaine do. But recent studies on animals and humans suggest that long-term Ecstasy users do risk becoming addicted to the drug. A report in 2001 found that 60 percent of the Ecstasy users that researchers followed showed signs of addiction.

Then, in the 1900s, new drugs came onto the market promising miracle cures for many things, from the common cold to serious diseases. These drugs did not provide the cures they promised. Some of them led to addictions because they were made with dangerous drugs, such as cocaine and opium. As a result, the U.S. Congress created new laws about drugs.

One new law required drug makers to list all of the ingredients in the drugs they made. Another law required drug makers to provide proof to support the promises they made about what a drug could do. In 1970, the U.S. Congress passed the Controlled Drugs Act. This act created five schedules, or categories, for drugs.

The federal Food and Drug Administration (FDA) decides which schedule a drug belongs in. They base their decisions on things such as:

- The likelihood that people will abuse the drug
- The likelihood that people will develop an addiction to the drug
- The drug's healing value or medical use
- The drug's harmfulness

Drugs that are the most likely to be abused and have no recognized healing value are Schedule 1 drugs. Schedule 5 drugs are the least harmful. Schedule 2, 3, and 4 drugs fall somewhere in between Schedule 1 and 5 drugs. Lawmakers use the schedules to decide how strict the punishments should be for making, delivering, and selling certain drugs. All drugs used in the United States have an assigned schedule. Ecstasy has been a Schedule 1 drug since 1988.

U.S. Drug Schedules

Schedule	Examples	Qualities
1	• Ecstasy • Heroin • LSD • Magic mushrooms • Marijuana	• Is likely to be abused • Has no accepted medical use • Has no safety guidelines for use
2	• Amphetamines • Cocaine • Codeine • Fentanyl • Ritalin	• Is likely to be abused • Has an accepted medical use, but there are strict rules about how it should be used • May lead to addictions that are very difficult to recover from
3	• Ketamine • Steroids	• Is less likely to be abused than Schedule 1 or 2 drugs • Has an accepted medical use • May lead to addictions that are somewhat difficult to recover from
4	• Rohypnol • Valium • Xanax	• Is less likely to be abused than Schedule 1, 2, or 3 drugs • Has an accepted medical use • May lead to addictions that are fairly easy to recover from
5	• Cough syrups with codeine	• Is less likely to be abused than other drugs • Has an accepted medical use • May lead to mild addictions that are easier to recover from than addictions to other drugs

Illegal and International

Most teenagers buy Ecstasy from a friend or someone they know, so buying this drug may seem like a harmless and safe act. But the truth is that buying just one tablet of Ecstasy contributes to an illegal and hidden business. It is a business that the law takes very seriously.

Ecstasy tablets often contain a variety of drugs. None of these drugs are allowed in the United States. Most of Europe doesn't allow these drugs either. But there are some countries that have more relaxed laws about drugs. The Netherlands is one of these countries. In The Netherlands, it is legal to make Ecstasy. Most of the world's Ecstasy comes from there.

Ecstasy is made illegally in many other places. Illegal Ecstasy labs are a big business. A typical Ecstasy lab produces 140,000 to 210,000 tablets per day. Given that the price of one tablet of Ecstasy is about $20, labs can create over $400,000 worth of illegal drugs in one day.

Once the tablets are made, they are delivered near and far. Ecstasy from other countries enters the United States in many different ways. Sometimes it is mailed, using express mail services, or shipped on an airplane that delivers mail and packages. Sometimes people carry it with them onto a passenger airplane. Most drugs enter the United States through the cities of Los Angeles, New York, and Miami and then find their way to nearly every city and town.

Attempts to Stop the Spread

The U.S. Drug Enforcement Administration (DEA) works to stop the delivery of illegal drugs in the United States, including Ecstasy. DEA operations aimed at stopping the spread of Ecstasy include:

- Operation Bad Vibe. In 1999, DEA agents seized large amounts of drugs from a rave-party promotion group in Arkansas. More than 50 people were arrested.

- Operation Rave I and Rave II. In 2001, DEA agents seized 7 million tablets of Ecstasy. Nearly 250 people were arrested.

- Operation Candy Box. From 2001 to 2004, DEA agents shut down several illegal drug labs and seized large amounts of drugs that were being delivered to 19 U.S. and Canadian cities. More than 130 people were arrested.

- Operation Triple Play. In 2006, DEA agents seized 50,000 tablets of Ecstasy, worth over one million dollars from a group that had been selling Ecstasy from Canada in the United States. There were 19 arrests.

Other operations are likely in progress. But the public won't learn about them until after they are finished.

Dealing with Criminals

DEA workers report more and more violence in the Ecstasy business, including violence between drug gangs. When DEA workers seize Ecstasy from drug dealers, they almost always find and seize weapons, too.

The number of people in jail for drug-related crimes continues to increase. Currently, more than 30 percent of the prisoners in state jails are there because of drug crimes. In federal jails, 60 percent of the prisoners are there because of drug crimes.

People who are arrested for using, holding, making, buying, or selling Ecstasy may spend up to 10 years in jail.

Scared Straight: Angela's Story

Angela, a 19-year-old college freshman, was studying to become a doctor. She was arrested for having five tablets of Ecstasy in her possession. This was in Louisiana, where the felony of possession is punishable by up to five years in jail.

The police stopped me for a speeding ticket, and the little bag of pills fell right out of my purse. They arrested me on the spot. They took me down to the police station and booked me for possession of Ecstasy, a felony.

With a felony arrest, I could be thrown out of school. It would be difficult, if not impossible, to get into medical school with a criminal record. I couldn't believe my dream of becoming a doctor was going to end.

Luckily for Angela, because this was her first arrest, she was given the option of doing a counseling and drug-testing program for six months, instead of going to jail. Angela did the program and met all the requirements. The charges against her were dropped.

4 Choosing a Drug-Free Life

THE SIMPLE TRUTH IS THAT IT IS NOT SAFE TO TAKE Ecstasy even once—and certainly not on a regular basis. Using Ecstasy causes changes in your brain and body that can make you sick. An overdose can kill you. Ecstasy can be habit-forming, or even addictive. Often, after a while, users need more and more of the drug to achieve the same high. Also, quitting can be very painful while the body adapts to the change. Furthermore, Ecstasy is an illegal drug. If you are caught with even a single tablet, you can be sent to jail.

Despite these facts, you may know people who have tried Ecstasy. You may know people who do Ecstasy regularly. You may be one of these people yourself.

One of the first steps toward breaking free of a drug habit is to talk with a counselor.

Why do young people risk their health and freedom for a drug? Some teens may simply not know enough about the dangers of using Ecstasy. But for many, a bad habit like drug abuse usually starts with fear or pain. The pain may come from unhappiness at school or with family. It may come from the demands of growing up. Peer pressure, or the fear of not fitting in, leads many teens to use drugs. Whatever the reason, many people have come to regret experimenting with or using dangerous drugs, like Ecstasy.

Starting Over

Obviously, the best choice is to avoid taking Ecstasy or any illegal drug. But people do not always make the best choices. And a few bad choices can lead to a few big problems.

The first step in solving a drug problem is to admit that there is a problem. If you or someone you know is using Ecstasy, you should talk with a doctor or counselor. Talking with a counselor can help people figure out why they are using drugs. A counselor or doctor can also help develop a treatment plan.

Programs such as Narcotics Anonymous (NA) help many users quit. NA is an international group of recovering drug addicts—people who are in the process of giving up drugs. Members meet regularly to support each other through the twelve steps of recovery. One step is to ask for forgiveness from people the NA member has hurt as a result of his or her drug use. Another step is to help other drug addicts who want to recover.

Struggling Back: Stella's Story

Stella is a 22-year-old college graduate. During high school, she used Ecstasy on a regular basis. When she saw the effect that her drug use was having on her health and her family life, she decided to stop using. She found that quitting Ecstasy was more difficult than she expected. It took about six months to get over the side effects of the drug. Stella still struggles with the effects that the drug abuse had on her emotions, but her life is looking better all the time.

I only felt "normal" when I was high. I thought I could only be myself on X.

I thought I could just go "cold turkey," so to speak. But I felt awful all the time—tired, anxious. Then my doctor suggested going to teen Narcotics Anonymous meetings to get another perspective and a chance to talk about what I was going through.

I was embarrassed at first, but after awhile I felt relieved. I wasn't alone, and there was no shame in what happened to me.

The short release from reality that Ecstasy provides does not outweigh the many costs of using an illegal drug. People who use illegal drugs like Ecstasy spend time feeling sick and unbalanced when the drug wears off. They often have to steal to pay for their drug habit. Many lie to keep their drug use a secret from friends and family. In addition, there is the risk of overdose and death. Ecstasy has contributed to more than 160 deaths.

Many people who quit using Ecstasy need to find new ways to handle the stresses of life. It is important to remember that this is possible and that drug abuse is treatable. Bad habits can be replaced by good ones.

Knowing more about the dangers of Ecstasy and other illegal drugs can help you make better choices. It helps you influence others to make good choices, too. This is an important way to protect your future and live a happy, drug-free life.

Friends can help each other get or stay drug-free.

GLOSSARY

addiction: A pattern of behavior based on the body or mind's need for a drug or activity.

anxiety: Feelings of uneasiness, worry, uncertainty, and fear that come from thinking about something that feels dangerous. Anxiety may be a normal reaction to a real danger, or it may occur when no real danger exists.

club drugs: Illegal drugs that are popular at dance clubs and raves.

depression: Feelings of sadness and despair, along with slowed thinking, appetite changes, sleeping problems, aches and pains, and not being able to feel pleasure.

designer drug: A drug made to give a desired high or to avoid laws against existing drugs.

dose: The amount of a drug that is to be taken at one time.

ecstasy: A state of feeling great joy and delight.

empathetic: Being aware of and relating to another person's feelings and experiences.

felony: A serious crime, such as murder or burglary, which is commonly punished in the United States with jail time.

hallucinogens: Drugs that change the user's experience of the world around him or her or that cause the user to see, hear, taste, smell, or feel things that are not real.

nerve fibers: Thread-like extensions of nerve cells.

neurotransmitters: Chemicals that send nerve signals. When an imbalance among the neurotransmitters occurs, emotional and physical symptoms result.

overdose: Symptoms that occur when someone takes or gets too much of something, usually a drug.

rave: An all-night dance party.

stimulants: Drugs that increase alertness, attention, and energy and raise blood pressure. They also speed up breathing and heart rate.

traumas: Experiences that create shock or emotional pain that is difficult to forget or recover from.

FIND OUT MORE

Books

Fitzhugh, Karla. *Ecstasy: What's the Deal?* Chicago: Heinemann, 2005.

Karson, Jill. *Club Drugs*. New York: Referencepoint, 2007.

Klosterman, Lorrie. *The Facts about Drugs and the Body*. New York: Marshall Cavendish, 2008.

Kuhn, Cynthia, Scott Swartzwelder, and Wilkie Wilson. *Buzzed: The Straight Facts about the Most Used and Abused Drugs from Alcohol to Ecstasy*. 3rd ed. New York: W. W. Norton, 2008.

LeVert, Suzanne. *The Facts about Ecstasy*. New York: Marshall Cavendish, 2005.

Lane, Stephanie. *Drug Education Library: Ecstasy*. New York: Lucent, 2005.

Lookadoo, Justin. *The Dirt on Drugs*. Grand Rapids: Revell, 2008.

Websites

Adolescent Substance Abuse Knowledge Base:
Ecstasy (MDMA)—Club Drugs
http://www.adolescent-substance-abuse.com/signs-ecstasy.html

Focus Adolescent Services: Ecstasy (MDMA)
http://www.focusas.com/Ecstasy.html

Narcotics Anonymous World Services
http://www.na.org

The National Institute on Drug Abuse (NIDA)
for Teens: Ecstasy
http://teens.drugabuse.gov/facts/facts_xtc1.php

INDEX

Page numbers for photographs and illustrations are in **boldface**.